Toe-Up Techniques
for Hand-Knit Socks
REVISED EDITION

Janet Rehfeldt

Toe-Up Techniques for Hand-Knit Socks,
Revised Edition
Text © 2008 by Janet Rehfeldt
Illustrations © 2008 by Timothy Maher

That Patchwork Place® is an imprint of
Martingale & Company®.

Martingale & Company
20205 144th Ave. NE
Woodinville, WA 98072-8478 USA
www.martingale-pub.com

Printed in China
13 12 11 10 09 08   8 7 6 5 4 3 2 1

Library of Congress Cataloging-in-Publication Data is available upon request.

ISBN: 978-1-56477-917-5

Dedication

To my family for all of their support, and to the memory of Elsie Downs, my grandmother, who never went anywhere without a ball of yarn, needle, or hook.

Mission Statement

Dedicated to providing quality products and service to inspire creativity.

Credits

President & CEO: Tom Wierzbicki
Editorial Director: Mary V. Green
Managing Editor: Tina Cook
Technical Editor: Karen Costello Soltys
Copy Editor: Liz McGehee
Design Director: Stan Green
Production Manager: Regina Girard
Illustrator: Tim Maher
Cover & Text Designer: Adrienne Smitke
Photographer: Brent Kane

Contents

Introduction

Making socks from the toe up is my favorite way of knitting or crocheting socks. There's practically no finishing work and no grafting toes, and custom fitting a sock worked from the toe up to the cuff is easier than fitting a sock worked from the cuff downward. The short-row heel is similar to commercial sock heels and is a bit shorter and narrower than a heel flap with gusset. Once you get the hang of knitting short-row heels, toe-up may become your favorite method of knitting socks, too. However, personal preference will always prevail, and you should knit your socks in your favorite manner.

I have always loved having choices; therefore, in this book I have given multiple ways of casting on, making increases, working with short-row wraps, and binding off. For those who prefer a heel flap and gusset over the short-row heel, I didn't leave you out; I have included a very good version of working a reverse heel flap with gusset for your toe-up socks.

In this updated and revised edition of this book, I've added some additional patterns, illustrations, and photographs. I hope you enjoy the technique of knitting your socks from the toe up as much as I have enjoyed putting this resource together for all the wonderful sock knitters out there. Happy knitting!

—Janet Rehfeldt

The Anatomy of Socks

Socks knit from the toe up can be worked with either a short-row heel or with a heel flap and gusset. Each has a distinct look.

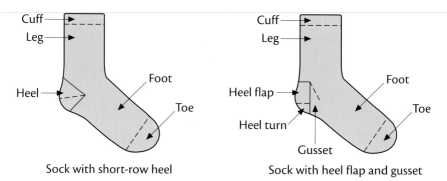

Sock with short-row heel   Sock with heel flap and gusset

Before You Begin

Before you dive into the techniques of knitting your socks from the toe up, this section will help you choose yarn and decide what size sock to knit. It will also explain the tools you need (or may want) to make your socks, as well as the ins and outs of working with double-pointed needles.

Sock yarns come in a large variety of styles, colors, and fiber contents.

Sock Yarns

When it comes to choosing sock yarn you will find a cornucopia of choices at your local yarn shop, ranging from solids to stripes to self-patterning colors. Yarns designed specifically for making socks usually have some nylon or polyamide in them and there are even those with elastic. When using a yarn with no nylon or polyamide content, you may want to knit elastic thread or Woolly Nylon serger thread into the cuff. If you choose to reinforce the heel and toe area, reinforcement yarn is available in a wide range of colors, and some companies include a package of reinforcement yarn for knitting together with their sock yarns as you work the heels and toes. If you have allergies to particular fibers, be sure to check the fiber content on the label, as even some of the cotton sock yarns may contain some wool or other fiber.

Choosing Your Size

One of the greatest benefits of knitting socks from the toe up is that you can try them on as you knit. Toe-up socks are often referred to as "knit to fit" or "until the yarn runs out" socks. You knit the toe increases until the sock toe fits the foot to the base of the little toe. You knit the foot until the sock fits to just below the ankle bone. After working the heel, you knit the leg and cuff until they reach the length you want—or until you run low on yarn.

To measure a foot for socks, first measure the circumference of the foot at the base of the little toe (A). Then measure the circumference of the foot at the widest point (B). Use these measurements to determine when to stop toe increases and if you need to increase the foot area. Your sock should be approximately ½" narrower than the foot measurements.

Next, while the person is standing, measure the length of the foot from the back of the heel to the tip of the longest toe (C). Use this measurement to know when to begin the heel; work the foot portion until it is approximately 2" shorter than the length of the foot.

When knitting toe-up socks from a specific pattern with multiple sizes, choose the size that is closest to the foot-circumference measurement. If your foot measurement is between sizes, choose the size that will give you the fit you want: smaller for a snug fit, larger for a loose fit. Hand-knit socks have a degree of stretch, so you do not knit them to the exact length of the foot. The finished foot length should be approximately ¾" to 1" shorter than the foot.

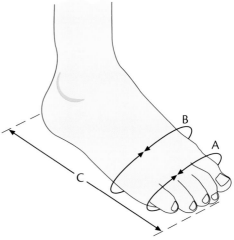

Where to measure the foot

Tools

A set of double-pointed needles and some sock yarn will have you well on your way to knitting your socks. However, as well as the basic must-haves for your knitting bag, there are some nifty tools and gadgets that are not only helpful, but just totally cool.

A variety of tools, such as stitch markers, stitch holders, a row counter, a needle gauge, and a tape measure, will make your sock knitting easier.

Double-pointed needles (dpns) come in different lengths ranging from 3" to 12". I prefer using 6"-long needles when knitting socks. Some of the longer needles can become tangled and interfere with each other while you're trying to work. I like working with wooden birch or bamboo-double pointed needles for wool and wool blends but prefer coated aluminum needles for cotton. There are also plastic flexible needles that work quite well with most yarns. Use the needles that you are most comfortable with, at the length you find the easiest to handle. Although I prefer to knit my socks on double-pointed needles, for those of you who enjoy working with two circular needles, the techniques in this book will work for you as well.

Row counters can be handy when working your increases or decreases and for keeping track of pattern repeats. If using a circular row counter, don't keep it on the needles. Thread yarn through the row counter and tie it into a loop. Using a knitter's pin, pin it to the body of the sock.

Closed-ring stitch markers are handy when working lace or pattern repeats. They're also helpful when marking where to increase for reverse heel flap and gusset sections. If you are new to knitting socks, you can find great novelty

HINTS AND TIPS

I like to pin my row counter at the back of the foot between needles 1 and 3. I seem to always know where I am in my rounds this way.

stitch markers with the numbers 1, 2, and 3 on them to place on each needle if you have trouble remembering the placement of your needles. There are also specialty markers for indicating which types of increases and decreases to make.

Tape measures are a must for any knitter's bag. A tape measure marked with both inches and centimeters will help with taking measurements for fitting your socks as well as for measuring your gauge.

Small or medium-size stitch holders are helpful when working the heel stitches. Putting the front foot stitches onto a holder while working the heel stitches gives you flexibility and makes the heel easier to knit.

Scissors are needed to cut yarn ends. For traveling, yarn-cutter pendants are very handy.

Tapestry needles have large eyes and blunt ends, making them good for weaving in ends and for working a tubular or sewn bind off.

Double-Pointed Needles

Working with double-pointed needles is a bit different than working in the round on circular needles. At first, you may find that they can become tangled and are a bit cumbersome; however, with a bit of patience and practice I think you'll find that working with double-pointed needles can become quite easy. They come in packages of either four or five needles. I use four needles when knitting with double points, so all the information in this book is written using four needles.

HINTS AND TIPS

If you find that your tension is just a bit too loose or too tight, you can adjust and even out your work by replacing one of the needles with a needle that is one size smaller or larger. This smaller or larger needle migrates around the work as you knit in the round and can help keep your stitches even. This works best when using needles below size US 7 (4.50mm) and when there is only a .25mm difference between sizes.

Socks on Double-Pointed Needles

As I mentioned earlier, the patterns in this book are written for using four double-pointed needles. Three needles are used to hold the stitches while the fourth needle is used to work the stitches. This means that you'll be working in a triangular shape, and the stitches are divided with half of the stitches on one needle and the other half of the stitches split between the other two needles. The two needles (needles 1 and 3) with fewer stitches hold the back or sole of the sock, while the needle with the larger number of stitches (needle 2) holds the front or instep of the sock.

Once you are set up with your stitches on three needles and have the right side of the work facing you, you'll work the stitches on needle 1 (back left-half section of sock) with your fourth needle. When all the stitches on needle 1 have been worked, you'll use the now-empty needle to work the stitches on needle 2 (front foot stitches). When all the stitches on needle 2 have been worked, you'll use that empty needle to work the stitches on needle 3 (back right-half section of sock).

You're now knitting your sock in the round on double-pointed needles. Continue in this method, making sure the right side of the work is facing you, and working around and around.

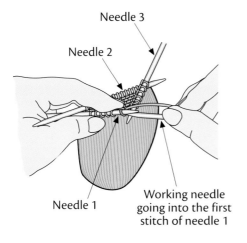

Needle 3

Needle 2

Needle 1

Working needle going into the first stitch of needle 1

HINTS AND TIPS

When working in the round with dpns, you may find that ladders or stranded gaps are forming between the stitches when you change from one needle to the next. To help eliminate this, after working the first stitch on each needle, pull it snug.

Casting On

At first, I always worked my toe-up socks with a figure-eight cast on. However, I usually need to tighten up the toe, stitch by stitch, once I am finished, so my preference now is for a closed-toe cast on. I have included the instructions for the figure-eight cast on along with two versions of a closed-toe cast on. Typically, the cast on ranges from 6 to 16 stitches, depending on the weight of yarn you use and how wide you want your toe. Try each one, then choose the type of cast on you are most comfortable with.

Figure-Eight Cast On

For this cast on, you'll need your yarn and two needles. You'll be wrapping figure-eights around the two needles.

1. Hold two needles parallel along with the tail of the yarn in your left hand. Place the yarn tail (leaving about a 6" tail) between the two needles. From between the two needles, pass the working end of the yarn over the top of the needle closest to you (the bottommost needle in the illustration); take the yarn under the bottom needle and *up between the two needles; then take the yarn up and over the top of the second needle (the topmost needle in the illustration); bring the yarn toward you, going down between the two needles, then over and under the bottommost needle.*

   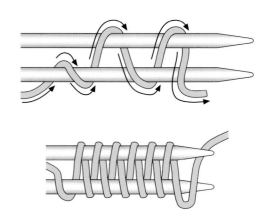

2. Repeat this process from * to * until you have 8 loops on both needles, counting the first tail wrap as a stitch and ending with the last wrap over the needle farthest from you. Allow the end of the yarn tail to hang without twisting it into the stitches or tying it off.

3. To knit the loops, pivot the needles away from you so that you are working into the loops on the bottom needle. Knit the first set of stitches through the front of the loop as you would make a normal knit stitch. The last loop on the needle is part of the tail, which is just looped over the needle; knit into as if it was a full stitch.

   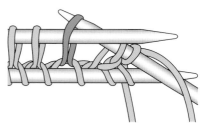

4. Pivot the needles to work into the loops on the other needle. This next set of stitches needs to be knit through the back of the loop as they will be twisted or the "wrong way" on the needle.

   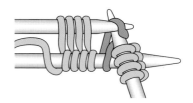

Note: If the stitches are loose, you can tighten them after several rounds of the toe have been knit or when the sock is finished by pulling up on the strands one by one until the stitches come together to the same size as your other knit stitches.

To add the third needle, knit half the stitches from the first needle (this becomes needle 3). Adding a needle, knit the remaining half of the stitches (this will become needle 1.) Knit all the stitches on the other needle; this is now needle 2 (the front foot stitches). Knit the stitches on needle 3 once more to get into the correct needle order for working your sock. You are now at the center of the back foot stitches, which will be the beginning of your rounds. See page 9 for an illustration of needle order.

Closed-Toe Cast Ons

Closed-toe cast ons are by far my favorite method for working socks from the toe up. Before beginning the closed-toe cast on, you need to get your first set of stitches onto the needle. The two closed-toe cast-on methods use a long-tail cast on (also referred to as the double-tail, fly-cast, or slingshot method), so lets review that first.

Long-Tail Cast On

Make a loop with a slipknot and place the loop on the needle. Holding the needle in your right hand, bring the thumb and forefinger of your left hand between the two tails of the yarn and hold onto both tails of the yarn with that hand. Continuing to hold onto the yarn tails, bring the needle down between your thumb and forefinger. The needle will be over the yarn tails, forming loops on your thumb and forefinger, and you will have what looks like a slingshot.

Following the arrows in the illustration, bring the needle under the yarn on your thumb, up along the thumb, over the top and back under the yarn on your forefinger, and then down through the yarn on your thumb. Pull up a bit on the yarn tails to form the first stitch, but don't pull too tightly. Continue to work in this manner until you have the number of stitches you need. You may have to reposition your thumb and forefinger a few times before you get the hang or flow of the cast on.

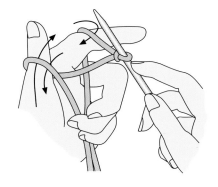

Closed-Toe Cast On 1

This cast-on method is done by working into the purl bump of each stitch. It creates a very smooth toe on the inside of the sock, which feels good on the foot. The beginning of the toe has small vertical stitches between the first two rounds, but depending on the needle size and yarn used, you might have a hard time seeing them, so it's still a nice-looking toe.

1. Using the long-tail method, cast on 8 stitches and knit 1 row. Turn the work and, working across half of the stitches, knit into the purl bumps of each stitch, placing each new stitch onto a second needle.

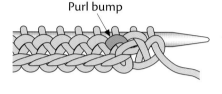

Purl bump

2. When you have knit half of the stitches, begin using a third needle to work into the purl bumps of the remaining 4 stitches. Turn the work and knit all 8 stitches off the original needle, using only one needle to knit them (this will be the front of the foot, needle 2).

3. To get to the center back of the foot so that the beginning of your rounds for your sock is needle 1, you now need to knit the stitches on the next needle (needle 3). You should now be at the center back of the foot and you're ready to begin increases at the side edges for toe shaping

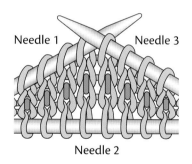

Needle 1   Needle 3

Needle 2

Closed-Toe Cast On 2

1. Using the long-tail method, cast on 10 stitches, knit 1 row, and turn. Working along the bottom of the cast on, knit into the bottom or base of the first stitch, now knit into the bottom two loops (not the purl bump) of the cast on as

shown. You are actually working between the knitted stitches. You work into what appears to be a chain stitch, placing each new stitch onto a second needle (fig. A).

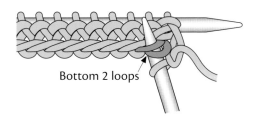

Bottom 2 loops

Fig. A

2. Knit half the stitches onto one needle (this will be needle 3, containing the right half of the back of the foot).

3. Using a third needle, knit the other half of the stitches onto the new needle (this will be the left half of the back of the foot, needle 1) (fig. B).

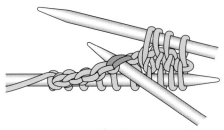

Fig. B

4. Turn the work and knit all 10 stitches from the original needle, using only one needle (this will be needle 2 with the front foot stitches). To get to the center of the back of the foot so that the beginning of your rounds for your sock is needle 1, you now need to knit the stitches on the next needle (needle 3). You should now be at the center back of the foot and you can begin increases at the side edges for toe shaping (fig. C).

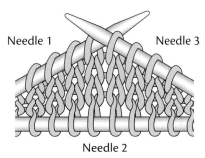

Needle 1   Needle 3

Needle 2

Fig. C

HINTS AND TIPS

For a smoother feel on the inside of the toe, once you are familiar with version 2 of the closed-toe cast on, try working it directly off the long-tail cast on without knitting a row first.

Shaping the Toe and Working the Foot

Once you've completed the cast on, you are ready to begin increasing for your toe shaping. As with casting on, there are several methods of increasing. You want your toe increases to be symmetrical, so you'll need to work left-slanting increases and right-slanting increases in the proper places. Just remember this mantra: When you are at the end of a needle, work a left-slanting increase. When you are at the beginning of a needle, work a right-slanting increase.

I've included three different ways of working increases. Try each and pick the increase that you find works best for you or that has the finished look you want for your toe shaping.

Raised Increases

Also known as strand increases, these increases are worked into the strand or horizontal bar that is located between two stitches.

Left-Slanting Raised Increase

Insert the left-hand needle from front to back under the horizontal bar between the last stitch worked and the next stitch, and lift the bar onto the left needle. Knit into the back of the stitch.

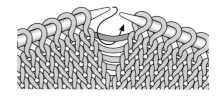

Right-Slanting Raised Increase

Insert the left-hand needle from back to front under the horizontal bar between the last stitch worked and the next stitch, and lift the bar onto the left needle. Knit into the front of the stitch.

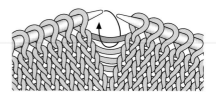

14

Yarn-Over or Closed-Eyelet Increases

These increases are similar in appearance and method to the raised increases. They are very nice looking and seem to give me the most consistency in look and size of my increased stitches.

Left-Slanting Yarn Over

Wrap the yarn over the needle from back to front. On the next round, knit into the front of the stitch to twist the stitch so you don't leave a hole or eyelet.

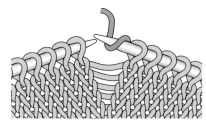

Right-Slanting Yarn Over

Bring the yarn forward, yarn over the needle from front to back. On the next round, knit into the back of the stitch to twist the stitch so you don't leave a hole or eyelet.

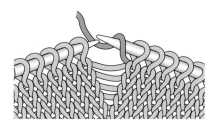

Lifted Increases

Rather than using the strand or bar between the stitches, these increases are worked into the back or side of a previous stitch. The increased stitches are quite smooth, but if you pull them too tight, they can pucker your toe shaping.

Left-Slanting Lifted Increase

With the left-hand needle, working from the back toward the front, pick up the side loop of the stitch just below the stitch just knit and knit into it. (You are working in the row below.)

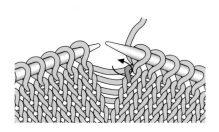

Insert the right-hand needle into
the back hump or purl bump of the
stitch below the next stitch to be
worked and knit into it. (You are
working in the row below.)

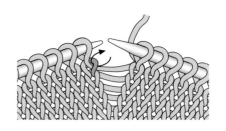

How Much to Increase

Once you have chosen your favorite increase, you'll work your increases on
every other round. Working an even round with no increases gives you a
nicely shaped and rounded toe. This is also where "fit as you knit" begins to
come into play. Keep trying on your sock toe until it reaches to just above the
base of your little toe. It should fit
your foot (or the foot of the person
you are making the socks for)
snugly but not tightly. If you are
working from a specific pattern,
work your toe increases until you
have the number of stitches in the
pattern that best fits your foot.

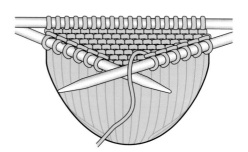

HINTS AND TIPS

*When your sock reaches about halfway between the toe and your
ankle, place half the front foot stitches onto a holder or another needle
when trying on your sock for fit. This will help you avoid breaking the
needles or injuring your foot.*

Sock Foot

Once you have finished the toe increasing so that the sock toe fits the foot
and/or has the number of stitches required in your written pattern, it's time to
move on to the foot of your sock.

The foot of the sock is knit in the round with the right side facing you until it reaches just below the bottom of the ankle bone or is approximately 2" shorter than the foot measurement taken from the back of the heel to the tip of the longest toe while standing.

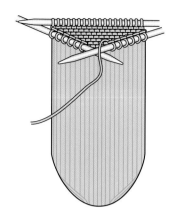

HINTS AND TIPS

In general, knitting is worked from the bottom up, which means that motif patterns are written to follow that knitting direction. So, when working a sock from the top down, you have to flip your pattern when you're working a motif or Spot the Dog will be standing on his head.

However, when knitting socks from the toe up, you don't have to flip a charted pattern because you are working from the bottom up toward the top. Therefore, any patterned design you choose will automatically be right side up without having to adjust it. This means that lace patterns will also appear as intended and you don't have to alter them.

Working Short-Row Heels

The heel of a sock is normally worked on half the total number of stitches on your sock. In other words, if you have 48 stitches, your heel would be worked on 24 stitches. Toe-up socks are generally knit using a short-row heel; however, the option of working a reverse heel flap and gusset is covered on page 28.

Short-row heels are most like those on commercial socks in shape and fit. The heel is worked back and forth, and you decrease by using shortened knit and purl rows. You knit or purl to a certain point on the heel stitches, and then stop and turn the work, leaving the remaining stitches of that row unworked—thus the term "short row."

You continue working these shortened rows until you have one-third of the original heel stitches left to work. You then begin to reknit or repurl the stitches that were left unworked, increasing back to the original number of heel stitches by working one additional stitch on each row.

Instructions are given for three ways of working a short-row heel: working double wraps, working single wraps, and working without wraps. Typically, I prefer to work double wraps when using very fine yarns, single wraps when using worsted-weight yarns, and the Japanese-pick method that uses no wraps when using even bulkier yarns, but the choice is really yours.

Short rows can leave holes or gaps in the work when you turn your work before the end of a row is completed, leaving the remaining stitches unworked. There are several methods of eliminating these holes or gaps in the work. In a double wrap, you wrap the stitches as you turn the work on both the decrease and increase sections. In a single wrap, you wrap only on the increase section. This pulls in the stitch that's being left unworked and closes the gap between the unworked stitch and the stitch next to it. The other method, the "pick method," is covered in "Short Rows without Wraps" on page 22.

Heel Decreases

1. Working only the heel stitches, knit the stitches on needle 1 to the last 2 stitches, bring your yarn to the front of the work, and slip 1 stitch purlwise from the left needle to the right needle (fig. A).

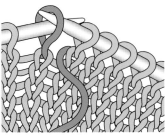

Fig. A

2. Return the working yarn to the back of the work (fig. B) and slip the stitch back onto the left needle. You didn't knit the stitch; you just wrapped the yarn around it to eliminate holes. You have 2 stitches that are not knit on needle 1 (the stitch you wrapped and the last stitch on the needle).

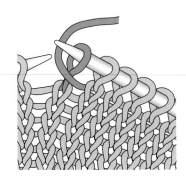

Fig. B

3. Turn your work. You still have those 2 stitches unworked, and now they are on the right-hand needle that you will use to purl back across needle 1.

4. Purl back across needle 1 and continue to purl across needle 3 (the other side of the heel) until there are 2 stitches left on needle 3. This time, put the yarn to the back of the work and slip the next stitch purlwise onto the right-hand needle (fig. C).

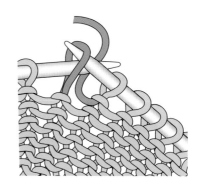

Fig. C

5. Pass the yarn between the needles to the front of the work (fig. D) and slip the same stitch back onto the left-hand needle.

6. You now have 4 stitches not worked: the 2 you didn't knit in row 1 and the 2 you didn't purl in row 2. Each time you knit or purl a row, work 1 less stitch,

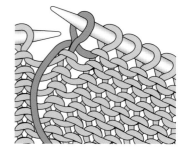

Fig. D

slipping and wrapping that stitch and leaving it unknit or unpurled until you have only the center one-third of the heel stitches that are actually knit, and all the rest of the stitches on both sides of the center stitches have been slipped and wrapped (or put on hold).

HINTS AND TIPS

To make life easier while working the heel, I put all the stitches from needle 2 (the front foot stitches) onto a stitch holder. I also work the stitches from both needles 1 and 3 (the heel section or back of the foot) onto just one needle and work it that way. It can be less confusing than trying to count worked and unworked stitches on two needles plus the one you are using to knit or purl them with. Then, when I've totally fin-ished the heel through all the increasing and decreasing, I redistribute the stitches back onto the correct needles.

The illustration at right shows the decrease section of the heel, complete with center heel stitches still in work while stitches on each side of the center have been slipped and wrapped.

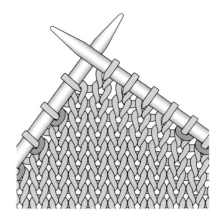

Heel Increases

After the heel decreases have been completed, you'll reverse the process and knit or purl one slipped and wrapped stitch per row until you've reworked all the stitches from the heel section. To hide the wraps when bringing the slipped stitches back up to work, you work the wrap and stitch together.

As you rework the original slipped and wrapped stitches, you will again wrap the next stitch each time you turn the work. So while you're returning the slipped stitches into worked stitches, you will actually have two wraps per stitch.

1. Knit up to the closest slipped stitch; then knit that stitch with the wrap together as 1 stitch.
2. Slip and wrap the next stitch; turn the work.
3. Purl back across to the closest slipped stitch; purl the stitch and wrap together as 1 stitch.
4. Slip and wrap the next stitch; turn the work.
   Continue working in this manner, repeating steps 1–4, until you have reworked all slipped and wrapped stitches.

Working the First Wraps

On the very first stitch you knit or purl back into work, there will be only one wrap. Lift the stitch onto the right-hand needle. On the knit side, lift the stitch as if to purl; on the purl side, lift the stitch as if to knit. Lift the wrap onto the right needle. Now slip both the wrap and the stitch onto the left-hand needle without changing their order. Knit or purl them together. Wrap the next stitch and turn the work.

Working the Remaining Wraps

Once you have completed the first knit and purl return rows, you'll be working with two wraps per stitch.

1. Lift the stitch onto the right-hand needle. On the knit side, lift the stitch as if to purl; on the purl side, lift the stitch as if to knit (fig. A).

2. Lift both wraps, one wrap at a time, onto the right-hand needle. Now slip both of the wraps and the stitch onto the left-hand needle. Do not change the order of the wraps and stitch when you slip them. Knit or purl the wraps and stitches together as 1 stitch (fig. B).

3. Wrap the next stitch and turn the work. On the next-to-last row on both the knit and purl sides, you will wrap the very last stitch on each needle before turning.

   When all the stitches have been knit or purled back into the work, your heel is finished (fig. C).

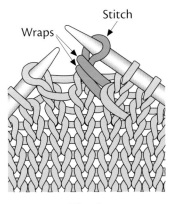

Fig. A

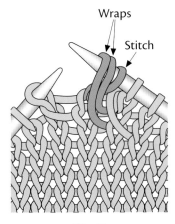

Fig. B

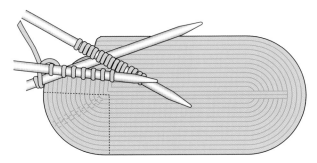

Fig. C

Single-Wrapped Short Rows

Single-wrapped short rows use the same principle as double-wrapped short rows; however, you wrap the stitches only once. This method can leave tiny holes or eyelets along the decrease line; however, the result is not as bulky as the double-wrapped short-row method.

To work single-wrapped short rows, don't slip and wrap the stitches when working the heel decreases; simply stop short and turn your work. You wrap the stitches only when turning the work while working the heel increases.

Short Rows without Wraps

You can work the short rows without wrapping the stitches and still eliminate the gaps or holes that are left when turning your work in mid-row. This is sometimes referred to as the pick, catch, or Japanese method. When putting the stitches out of work, do not slip and wrap the stitch when turning. When bringing your stitches back into work, you pick up the strand between two stitches in the row below and knit or purl the strand together with the stitch. This takes a bit of practice, but once you've done it a couple of times, instinct will take over and you'll know just where to pick up the strands to eliminate the holes.

Picking on Knit Rows

Work to the closest slipped stitch. Using the left-hand needle, pick up the strand between two stitches in the row below on the back side (purl side) of the work. Knit the strand together with the next knit stitch as one stitch. You might find it easier to have the purl side facing you when you pick up the strand onto the left-hand needle; then turn the work back to the knit side to knit the strand and stitch together as one as shown.

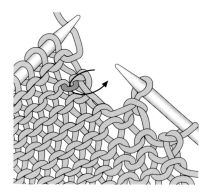

Picking on Purl Rows

Work to the closest slipped stitch. Using the left-hand needle, pick up the strand between two stitches in the row below, reverse the order of the lifted strand and the next stitch to be worked, and purl them together as one stitch.

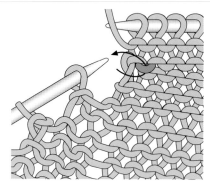

Working the Sock Leg and Cuff

Now that your heel is finished, you need to return to working in the round. If you split your front foot stitches onto two needles or put them onto a stitch holder, return them to a single needle so you're again working on three needles.

Sock Leg

At this point, you may find that you have a small hole where the heel joins the front of the foot. You can eliminate this in one of two ways, which are described below.

Closing the Gap: Method 1

One way to avoid a hole on each side of your sock is to pick up the strands between the front and back foot needles on the first full round of the leg.

1. Work up to the last stitch on needle 1, slip the stitch temporarily to the right-hand needle, pick up the strand between that stitch and the first stitch on needle 2 (front foot stitches), placing the strand onto needle 1. Slip both the strand and the stitch back to the left-hand needle and knit them together as 1 stitch.
2. Work the front foot stitches.
3. Lift the strand between the last stitch of needle 2 and the first stitch on needle 3 up onto needle 3. Knit the strand and the first stitch on needle 3 together as 1 stitch. If your hole is large, you will have to twist the strand before working it together with the stitch.

Closing the Gap: Method 2

Although both methods close the gap, I personally find the second method easiest to work, so it tends to be my method of choice.

When I get to the point in my heel where I have only one knit and one purl stitch left that I need to bring back into the work, I work the last two rows of the heel increases differently.

1. Ending with a purl row, turn to begin knitting the last knit row of the heel. When you have knit half the stitches of the heel, bring in another needle to knit the remaining heel stitches, making sure to pick up the wrap on the last knit stitch. (It is now needle 1.)
2. Do not turn and purl back. Instead, knit the front foot stitches in pattern onto one needle (remember you either split them onto two needles or put them onto a holder when you began the heel), making that again needle 2.

3. Now pick up the wrap, lifting it onto needle 3, and knit it together with the first stitch on needle 3. Work the remaining stitches on needle 3.

Finish the Leg

Work the leg section as you worked the foot section, in the round, until it is the height you wish your sock to be minus the height of your cuff. Remember to read your pattern instructions, as you may now be working all stitches in your stitch pattern, not just the instep stitches.

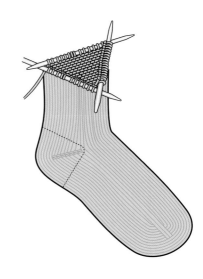

Sock Cuff

Cuffs are typically worked in either a K1, P1 ribbing or K2, P2 ribbing for 1½" to 2". If you have worked the leg using a pattern stitch, knit 1 round in stockinette stitch before beginning to work your ribbed cuff, to make a smooth transition. If your stitch count needs to be increased or decreased to accommodate the type of ribbing you want to knit, this knit transition round is the place to do any increases or decreases.

Binding Off

If you've worked a cuff in ribbing, you should bind off in the rib pattern, knitting the knit stitches and purling the purl stitches as you bind off. I generally like to use one needle size larger to work the stitches on the bind-off round, but if you have a tendency to bind off tightly, then use a needle two sizes larger to bind off your socks.

Simple Rib Bind Off

This is a good bind off for either K1, P1 or K2, P2 ribbing. Working slightly loosely, work the first stitch on needle 1, and work the next stitch in knit or purl as if you were continuing in pattern. Now with the left-hand needle, lift and pass the first stitch over the stitch just worked. Work the next stitch, and lift and pass the previous stitch over the stitch just worked. Continue working a stitch and passing the previous stitch over the stitch just worked until you have completed all the stitches. Leaving about a 6" tail for weaving in, cut the yarn and pull the tail through the last loop left.

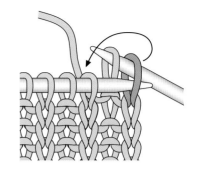

Suspended Rib Bind Off

This is a very stretchy bind off and adds a bit of give if you tend to bind off stitches tightly. The suspended bind off is worked similar to your basic rib bind off; however, when you lift the first stitch over the last worked stitch, don't drop the stitch off the left-hand needle. Work the next stitch, and then, when allowing the finished stitch to naturally go onto the right-hand needle, drop off that first stitch.

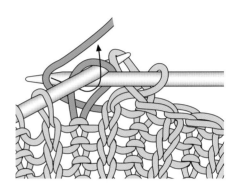

Sewn Bind Off

This bind off, also referred to as a grafted bind off, is a good, flexible bind off. You work into each stitch twice, mimicking the knit/purl stitches. The instructions below are for a cuff worked in a K1, P1 ribbing. When you finish the cuff, don't bind off or fasten off. Instead, cut the yarn, keeping a tail about four to five times the circumference of the sock.

Sewn Bind Off: Method 1

1. Thread the yarn tail into a tapestry needle. Assuming the first stitch on needle 1 is a knit stitch, insert the tapestry needle into the stitch as if to purl, *working between the first two stitches (the knit and purl), take the tapestry needle behind the knit stitch and insert it into the purl stitch as if to knit. Leave the stitches on the knitting needle.
2. Bring your yarn around to the front of the work at the end of the knitting needle, then insert the tapestry needle through the same knit stitch as if to knit, and slip the knit stitch off the knitting needle.
3. Bring the tapestry needle and yarn in front of the purl stitch and insert the needle into the next knit stitch as if to purl. Bring the tapestry needle

through the purl stitch as if to purl and slip it off the knitting needle.* Repeat from * to * around the work.

Note: Only slip a stitch off the knitting needle after you've worked into it twice with your tapestry needle. When all stitches have been slipped off the knitting needles, fasten off

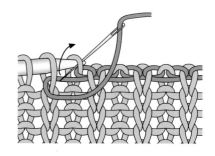

yarn. To work this bind off on K2, P2 ribbing, begin with a knit stitch, then rather than working the next purl stitch, work into the *next stitch* regardless of whether it's a knit or purl. Basically you're just sewing in and out of the stitches, always in the same order, no matter if they're knit or purled.

Sewn Bind Off: Method 2

This is similar to method 1 except that you separate your knit and purl stitches onto two needles and work off the two needles. This method is easiest on K1, P1 ribbing, but with a little practice, it's a great bind off for K2, P2 ribbing too.

1. Using two double-pointed needles and working only with those stitches on needle 1, place the knit stitches on one needle and the purl stitches on another needle as follows: Slip the first knit stitch onto one needle, and then place the next purl stitch onto the second needle. Holding the needles parallel, keep the knit stitches on the front needle and the purl stitches in back.

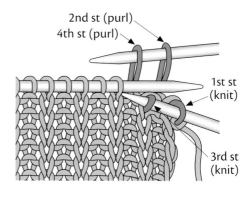

2nd st (purl)
4th st (purl)
1st st (knit)
3rd st (knit)

2. Thread the yarn tail into a tapestry needle.
3. Working with a knit stitch first, insert the tapestry needle into the first stitch on the front knitting needle as if to purl, pull the yarn through, and adjust the tension so that it's not tight but also not sloppy loose. (Note: If the first stitch is not a knit stitch, place it onto sock knitting needle 3 so that you begin with a knit stitch.)
4. Working from right to left (front to back), bring the tapestry needle through the back of the last stitch on needle 3. Pull the yarn through

snugly but not too tight, leaving the stitch on its own knitting needle. (You will work this stitch as the last stitch to be bound off.)

5. Insert the tapestry needle from right to left (front to back) through the front of the first purl stitch on the back knitting needle, and pull yarn through and leave the stitch on the knitting needle.

6. *Insert the tapestry needle from right to left (front to back) through the back of the first knit stitch and, in the same motion from right to left (front to back), through the next knit stitch on the front knitting needle. Slip the first knit stitch off the knitting needle and pull the yarn through, snugly but not tight.

7. Insert the tapestry needle into the first purl stitch on the back knitting needle from right to left (front to back), and slip the stitch off the knitting needle but keep it on the tapestry needle. Do not pull the yarn through.

8. Insert the tapestry needle from left to right (back to front) through the next purl stitch on the back needle, and pull the yarn through snugly but not tight.*

Repeat from * to *, separating additional knit and purl stitches onto two needles as needed. After you have worked about one third of your stitches, check the stretchiness of the work. If it's too loose or sloppy, tighten up slightly. If it's too tight, loosen up on your tension when pulling the yarn through the stitches.

For a K2, P2 ribbing, separate the knit and purl stitches from one sock needle onto two separate dpns and work the last purl stitch on needle 3 as listed above, leaving it on the knitting needle to be worked last.

1. Insert the tapestry needle into the first knit stitch knitwise, and insert the tapestry needle into the first purl stitch knitwise. *Insert the tapestry needle into the previously worked knit stitch purlwise and, in the same motion, insert the needle into the next knit stitch knitwise, allowing the first knit stitch to drop from the tip of the knitting needle.

2. Insert the tapestry needle into the previously worked purl stitch purlwise and, in the same motion, insert the tapestry needle into the next purl stitch knitwise, allowing the first purl stitch to drop from the tip of knitting needle.*

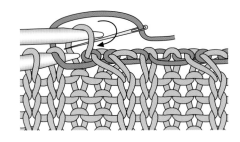

3. Rep from * to * until the first set of stitches is complete, and then transfer the next set of stitches and continue from * to * until all stitches are worked.

Working a Reverse Heel Flap and Gusset

Knitting a sock from the toe up does not mean that you always have to do a short-row heel. If you like the feel and shape of the heel flap and gusset associated with a traditional top-down sock, you're in luck. You can work your sock with a reverse heel flap and gusset section.

Socks knit with a reverse heel flap and gusset are worked the same as socks with a short-row heel from the cast on through the foot section until they reach to just below the ankle bone or are approximately 2" shorter than the total foot length.

Working the Gusset Increases and Instep

Because we are working in the reverse of a top-down sock, instead of decreasing at the instep and gusset section, we need to knit the instep even and *increase* to make a gusset section. Don't panic; you didn't miss anything. We haven't done the heel flap and turn yet. That comes later. When working from the toe up, the gusset increases are worked before creating the heel. You'll be increasing on the back of the foot stitches only, working two increases on each increase round and working one round even between the increase rounds. The front foot (instep) stitches are knit even without increasing.

Use your favorite method of making left- and right-slanting increases as you did for your toe. Starting with needle 1, knit up to the last stitch on the needle, work a left-slanting increase, and then knit the last stitch on the needle. Work needle 2 (instep stitches) in your foot pattern stitch without increasing. On needle 3, knit 1 stitch, work a right-slanting increase, and then knit the remaining stitches on needle 3. Knit one round without increasing.

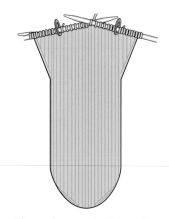

The markers on the illustration are just to show you the original center-back heel stitches located between the markers, and the gusset increases on either side of the markers.

Determining Gusset Width

Typically, each gusset section should be approximately 1¼" to 2" wide so that the sock fits around the heel and instep of your foot. If you have wide ankles, work your gusset section to the full 2" or even a bit wider. You don't want the gusset to be too wide, or the sock will be baggy. But if the gusset is too small, the sock will strangle your foot and ankle.

Using your stitch gauge, calculate how many stitches equal 1½" to 2" by multiplying the number of stitches per inch by the width you want your gusset section. For example, if you want a gusset section that measures 1½" and your stitch gauge is 7 stitches per inch, multiply 7 stitches x 1.5 inches to determine that you need to increase 10.5 stitches on each side of the heel.

When the number of stitches needed is a fraction of .5 or over (one-half a stitch or larger) I round up to the next whole number. In our example, I'd increase 11 stitches on each side of the heel to make the 1½" gusset section for each side of the heel.

If the number of stitches needed is less than .5, I simply don't worry about the fraction of a stitch. For example, if my calculations came out to 10.28 stitches, I'd round down to 10 stitches per gusset.

To better help you determine how wide to make your gusset, you can use this chart of average gusset widths:

Narrow-width foot	1¼"
Medium-width foot	1½ to 1¾"
Wide foot	1¾ to 2"
Extra-wide foot	2" or a bit wider

If you are working a gusset wider than 1¾", work the last three or four sets of increases on every round.

Working the Heel Turn

With the gusset and instep complete, it's time to work the heel turn, which is worked only on the original back foot stitches. It does not include the gusset increases. The heel turn is done by working short rows until one-third of the original heel stitches are left in work, while the other two-thirds have been slipped and wrapped, placing them out of work (or on hold).

The decrease section is worked the same way as for a regular short-row heel, but you'll put two stitches on hold for each knit and purl row rather than just one stitch. However, after completing the decreases, you'll bring all the knit and purl stitches back into work in just two rows, rather than increasing one stitch at a time and wrapping as you go. Begin your heel with a purl row.

1. To make working the heel turn easier, split the front foot (instep) stitches onto two needles. Working with one needle at a time on the front stitches, place a stitch marker at the beginning of the needle that is located after needle 1 of the back foot, and slip the increased gusset stitches from needle 1 onto that front foot needle.

2. Place a marker at the end of the front foot needle that comes just before needle 3 of the back foot and place the gusset stitches from needle 3 onto that front foot needle. You should have the original number of heel stitches on both needle 1 and needle 3 that you had before you began your gusset increases.

Heel Decreases

1. Begin working the short-row heel by knitting across needle 1 with needle 3. Turn the work and purl back to 2 stitches from the end. Following the instructions for wrapping short rows, wrap the next stitch and turn the work (see "Working Short-Row Heels" on page 17).

2. Knit back across the heel stitches to 2 stitches from the end; wrap and turn.

3. Purl back across the heel stitches to 2 stitches from the last wrapped stitch. Wrap the next stitch and turn. Knit back across the heel stitches to 2 stitches from the last wrapped stitch. Wrap the next stitch and turn.

4. Continue in this manner until only the center one-third stitches are left in work. For example, if you have 18 total heel stitches, you should have 6 stitches at the center of the heel still in work, with 6 stitches wrapped and held on each side of the center stitches.

Heel Increases

1. To bring the stitches back into work, purl back across the center stitches, then purl all the slipped and wrapped stitches (making sure to purl the wrap and stitch together as 1 stitch to avoid holes) up to the last stitch. Purl the last stitch together with 1 gusset stitch from the front needle.

2. Turn, slip 1 stitch purlwise, and then knit all the heel stitches (making sure to knit the wrap and stitch together as 1 stitch when you get to the wrapped stitches at the end of the needle, to avoid holes) up to the last stitch on the heel. Knit the last stitch together with 1 gusset stitch from the front foot needle (see "Working the First Wraps" on page 20).

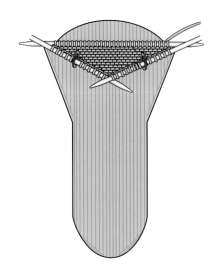

Creating the Heel Flap

The heel flap is knit in the same manner as a traditional basic heel flap; however, you now need to incorporate the gusset increases that were temporarily placed on the front foot needles. You'll still be working only with the back heel stitches and the gusset stitches. You won't be knitting the original front foot (instep) stitches.

Continue working with the needles as they are: one needle holding the heel stitches and two needles holding the front foot (instep) and gusset stitches.

Row 1: Slip 1 stitch, then purl across to the last heel stitch. Purl the last heel stitch together with the next gusset stitch from the front foot needle. Turn the work.

Row 2: *Slip 1 stitch, knit 1,* repeat from * to * to the last heel stitch. Knit the last heel stitch together with the next gusset stitch from the front foot needle. Turn the work.

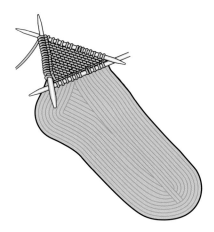

Repeat these last 2 rows, just like a normal heel flap, and work the last heel stitch together with 1 gusset stitch until all the gusset stitches have been worked. Then return to working in the round to knit the leg and cuff in the usual fashion.

Finishing the Leg and Cuff

Place all the front foot (instep) stitches onto one needle (needle 2), and split the back of the sock stitches onto two needles (needles 1 and 3) as before. The leg of the sock is worked in the same fashion as toe-up socks made with short-row heels (see page 17). Work the leg to the height that you desire minus the height of the cuff.

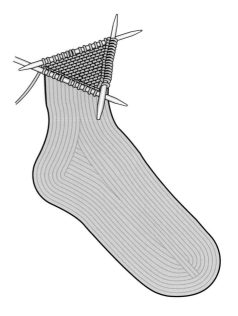

If you've worked a pattern stitch, knit one round in stockinette stitch before working your ribbed cuff for a smooth transition. If your stitch count needs to be adjusted to accommodate the type of ribbing you choose to knit, this knit transition round is the place to do any increases or decreases. Work your cuff to the desired height. A typical cuff length is 1½ to 2". Bind off using your method of choice, referring to "Binding Off" on page 24.

Projects

The following patterns are written in standard abbreviated format. All short-row heel instructions are written for working with wraps. If you choose to work single-wrap short rows or short rows with no wraps, refer to the short-row heels section beginning on page 17.

If there is an instruction you are unsure of, check the abbreviation list on page 61 and refer to the corresponding section in the book for that instruction. Example: M1L or M1R, which indicates you increase one stitch either as a left-slanting or right-slanting increase. If you are unsure or want to refresh your memory on right- and left-slanting increases, refer to the toe shaping section beginning on page 14.

Designer's Notes for All Patterns

- Each pattern is written for size narrow, with medium, wide, and extra-wide listed respectively in ( ) when instructions differ.
- Needles 1 and 3, with fewer stitches, represent the back or sole of the sock. Needle 2, with the larger number of stitches, represents the front or instep of the sock.
- Heels are worked on one-half of the total foot stitches. You may find it easier to work the heel by putting the front foot stitches on a stitch holder.
- If you are knitting both socks from one ball or skein of yarn, you may want to cut the yarn on your first sock, leaving a 4" to 6" tail for weaving in, and then put the stitches onto three stitch holders before you knit the cuff. Knit the second sock, and when both socks are the same height, check how much yarn you have left. You may have enough yarn to make your socks taller before working the cuffs.

Basic Toe-Up Socks

This stockinette-stitch sock pattern is great for working your way through all the basics of toe-up socks with short-row heels.

Finished Size

Circ. of foot (unstretched): 6¾ (7¾, 8⅞, 10)"
Circ. of leg (unstretched): 6¾ (7¾, 8⅞, 10)"
Height from floor to cuff: approx 7"

Materials

2 skeins of Kroy Socks from Patons (75% washable wool/25% nylon; 192 yds/ 175 m; 1.75 oz/50 g), color 54567 Paint Box (1)
Size US 2 (2.75 mm) double-pointed needles or size to achieve gauge
Stitch holder (optional)
Tapestry needle

Gauge

8.75 sts = 1" in St st

Cast On

Work figure-eight CO with 8 (10, 12, 14) wraps on each of 2 ndls or a closed-toe CO beg with 8 (10, 12, 14) sts. End with 16 (20, 24, 28) sts total after finished CO and with ndls in working order for knitting in the round. Divide sts as follows: 4-8-4 (5-10-5; 6-12-6; 7-14-7).

Toe Increases

Rnd 1 (inc. rnd): *Ndl 1:* knit to last 2 sts, K1, M1L, K1; *ndl 2:* K1, M1R, knit to last 2 sts, K1, M1L, K1; *ndl 3:* K1, M1R, knit rem sts (4 sts inc).

Rnd 2: Knit even.

Rep rnds 1 and 2, inc 4 sts per inc rnd, until you have a total of 60 (68, 80, 88) sts, divided as follows: 15-30-15 (17-34-17; 20-40-20; 22-44-22), or until toe fits foot snugly but not tightly just to base of little toe.

Foot

Knit even until sock fits just to bottom of ankle bone or until sock foot measures approx 2" less than total length of foot from heel to longest toe.

Short-Row Heel Decreases

Row 1: Work across ndl 1 to last 2 sts, wyif sl 1 st from LH ndl to RH ndl, wyib sl same st back to LH ndl. Turn work (wrap and turn complete).

Row 2: Purl across ndl 1 sts, and using same needle, purl across ndl 3 to last 2 sts, wyib sl 1 st from LH ndl to RH ndl, wyif sl same st back to LH ndl, turn.

Row 3: Knit to last 3 sts, sl and wrap next st as in row 1, turn.

Row 4: Purl across to last 3 sts, sl and wrap next st as in row 2.

Cont to work heel sts, slipping and wrapping an additional st each row until you have 10 (12, 14, 16) center sts rem that are knit, and 10 (11, 13, 14) sts that are wrapped on each side of center sts.

Short-Row Heel Increases

Refer to "Heel Increases" on page 20 as needed.

Row 1: Knit across center 10 (12, 14, 16) sts to closest wrapped st, K1 (knit st and wrap tog as 1 st), sl and wrap next st, turn.

Row 2: Purl across center 11 (13, 15, 17) sts to closest wrapped st, P1 (purl st and wrap tog as 1 st), sl and wrap next st, turn.

Cont to work heel sts, bringing 1 st back into work each row until you have worked all sts. On last 2 rows, knit across, wrap last st, turn, purl across, wrap last st, turn.

Knit each of these last 2 sts with their wraps tog as 1 st when you come to them on first rnd of the leg.

Leg and Cuff

If you placed the front sts on a holder, return them to ndl. You should have the same number of sts you began with before working the heel.

Return to working on 3 ndls. Knit even in the round until leg reaches 5" or desired height from bottom of the heel.

Work in K2, P2 rib for 2".

Finishing

Bind off *loosely*. Weave in all ends.

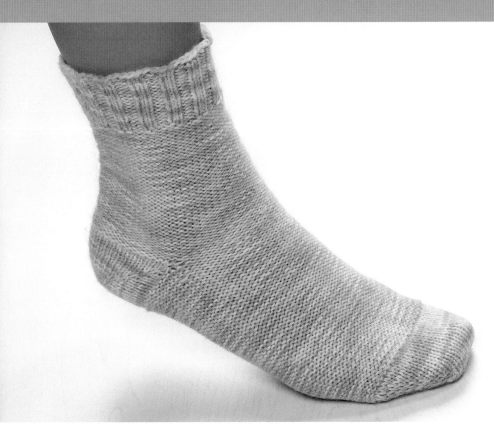

Sock shown was knit in Baby Boom from Fiesta yarns (100% extra-fine Superwash merino; 220 yds/201 m; 50 g) in color Vanilla.

Purled Toe-Up Socks

This purled version of the basic toe-up sock will feel wonderfully smooth on the bottom of your foot, whether you're walking about in shoes or just simply padding around the house in your stocking feet.

You can use the same Basic Toe-Up Socks pattern, but after the toe increases, purl all rounds rather than knitting them. Work the short-row heel in stockinette stitch.

If you don't enjoy purling in the round, after purling just 2 rounds, turn the sock inside out and begin to knit. Eliminate the first round's hole or gap created when turning the work by using the pick method on page 22, or slip and wrap the first stitch on the adjacent needle at the beginning of the first knit round. Turn the work back so the purl side is out to work the heel, purling 1 round and eliminating the hole or gap before working the heel. After the heel is finished, purl 2 rounds, turn the sock inside out, eliminate the hole or gap, and then knit all rounds for the leg.

Pebbles and Lace

This is one of my favorite socks. The cotton elastic yarn is easy to work with and makes this one of the most comfortable socks I own. The lace and seed-stitch pattern give the sock a simple yet sophisticated look.

Finished Size

Circ. of foot (unstretched): 6½ (7½, 8⅝, 9¾)"
Circ. of leg (unstretched): 6½ (7½, 8⅝, 9¾)"
Height from floor to cuff: approx 7"

Materials

2 (2, 2, 3) skeins of Fixation from Cascade Yarns [98.3% cotton/1.7% elastic; 186 yds (expanded)/100 yds (relaxed); 1.75 oz/50 g], color 2550 Lapis Blue 【2】
Size US 3 (3.25 mm) double-pointed needles or size to achieve gauge
Stitch holder (optional)
Tapestry needle

Gauge

29½ sts = 4"; 7⅜ sts = 1" in St st

Designer's Notes

- The bottom of the foot is knit in stockinette stitch while the top of the foot is patterned. When you begin the leg portion, begin all rounds with needle 2 (front foot needle) and end with needle 1.
- If you're custom fitting the sock, work toe increases to a multiple of 8 stitches so the pattern works out correctly. Divide the stitches onto 3 needles so that the front foot needle has a number divisible by 8. Even out the back stitches to only half the total number of stitches to work the heel, and then return to the original division of stitches to work the leg.

Cast On

For all sizes, work figure-eight CO with 10 wraps on each of 2 ndls or a closed-toe CO beg with 10 sts. End with 20 sts total after finished CO and with ndls in working order for knitting in the round. Divide as follows: 5-10-5.

Toe Increases

Rnd 1 (inc rnd): *Ndl 1:* knit to last 2 sts, K1, M1L, K1; *ndl 2:* K1, M1R, knit to last 2 sts, K1, M1L, K1; *ndl 3:* K1, M1R, knit rem sts (4 sts inc).

Rnd 2: Knit even.

Rep rnds 1 and 2, inc 4 sts EOR, until you have a total of 48 (56, 64, 72) sts. Divide as follows: 12-24-12 (16-24-16; 16-32-16; 20-32-20).

Note: The back heel stitches on the second and fourth sizes will be evened out to half the total stitches when working the heel.

Foot

Rnd 1: *Ndl 1:* knit; *ndl 2:* *K1, P1, rep from * across; *ndl 3:* knit.

Rnd 2: *Ndl 1:* knit; *ndl 2:* *P1, K1, rep from * across; *ndl 3:* knit.

Rnds 3–8: Rep rnds 1 and 2.

Rnd 9: *Ndl 1:* knit; *ndl 2:* *K1, YO, sl 1, K1, psso, K3, K2tog, YO, rep from * across; *ndl 3:* knit.

Rnds 10, 12, and 14: Knit all sts.

Rnd 11: *Ndl 1:* knit; *ndl 2:* *K2, YO, sl 1, K1, psso, K1, K2tog, YO, K1, rep from * across; *ndl 3:* knit.

Rnd 13: *Ndl 1:* knit; *ndl 2:* *K3, YO, sl 1, K2tog, psso, YO, K2, rep from * across; *ndl 3:* knit.

Rep rnds 1–14 until sock fits to bottom of ankle bone or until sock foot measures approx 2" less than foot from heel to longest toe, ending with rnd 14.

Short-Row Heel Decreases

For second and fourth sizes *only (56 and 72 sts):* Place 2 sts from each of ndls 1 and 3 onto ndl 2 before you begin the heel so you are working on 28 (36) sts.

Row 1: Work across ndl 1 to last 2 sts. Wyif sl 1 st from LH ndl to RH ndl, wyib sl same st back to LH ndl, turn (wrap and turn complete).

Row 2: Purl across ndl 1 and, using same ndl, purl across ndl 3 to last 2 sts, wyib sl 1 st from LH ndl to RH ndl, wyif sl same st back to LH ndl, turn.

Row 3: Knit to last 3 sts, sl and wrap next st as in row 1, turn.

Row 4: Purl across to last 3 sts, sl and wrap next st as in row 2, turn.

Cont to work heel sts, slipping and wrapping an additional st each row, until you have 8 (10, 12, 12) center sts that are knit and 8 (9, 10, 12) sts that are wrapped on each side of center sts.

Short-Row Heel Increases

When working sts with wraps, work st and wrap tog as 1 st. Refer to "Heel Increases" on page 20 as needed.

Row 1: Knit across center 8 (10, 12, 12) sts to closest wrapped st, K1 (knit st and wrap tog as 1 st), sl and wrap next st, turn.

Row 2: Purl across center 9 (11, 13, 13) sts to closest wrapped st, P1 (purl st and wrap tog as 1 st), sl and wrap next st, turn.

Cont to work heel sts, bringing 1 st back into work each row until you have worked all sts. On last 2 rows, knit across, wrap last st, turn, purl across, wrap last st, turn.

Knit each of these 2 sts tog with their wraps as 1 st when you come to them on the first rnd of the leg.

Leg and Cuff

If you placed the front sts on a holder, return them to ndl. You should have the same number of sts you began with before working the heel.

Return to working on 3 ndls. *On 56 and 72 sts only,* place 2 sts from each end of front foot ndl onto ndls 1 and 3. Divide sts as follows: 12-24-12 (16-24-16; 16-32-16; 20-32-20).

Work lace and seed patt st around entire leg portion, beg all rnds with front foot ndl 2. This is especially important when you beg the lace on rnd 9; you must beg patt with ndl 2.

Rnd 1: *K1, P1, rep from * around.

Rnd 2: *P1, K1, rep from * around.

Rnds 3–8: Rep rnds 1 and 2.

Note: Notice that when you end round 1 with a purl stitch that you also begin round 2 with a purl stitch. If you don't do this, you'll end up with a K1, P1 rib rather than a seed-stitch pattern.

Rnd 9: *K1, YO, sl 1, K1, psso, K3, K2tog, YO, rep from * around.

Rnds 10, 12, and 14: Knit all sts.

Rnd 11: *K2, YO, sl 1, K1, psso, K1, K2tog, YO, K1, rep from * around.

Rnd 13: *K3, YO, sl 1, K2tog, psso, YO, K2, rep from * around.

Rep rnds 1–14 three times or until leg is desired height from bottom of heel.

Work in K1, P1 rib for 2".

Finishing

Bind off *loosely*. Weave in all ends.

A Little Ruched

Slipped and tucked stitches along the leg section give this sock a ruched effect. It's especially pretty when used with a lightly patterned or solid-color yarn that shows off the pillowy sections and long slipped stitches.

Finished Size

Circ. of foot (unstretched): 6⅝ (7½, 8⅜, 9¼)"
Circ. of leg (unstretched): 6⅝ (7½, 8⅜, 9¼)"
Height from floor to cuff: approx 8½"

Materials

1 skein of Sockittome from Cherry Tree Hill (80% Superwash merino/20%
    nylon; 450 yds/411 m; 3.5 oz/100 g), color Cherry Blossom (1)
Size US 2 (2.75 mm) double-pointed needles or size to achieve gauge
2 stitch holders (optional)
2 stitch markers
Tapestry needle

Gauge

9 sts = 1" in St st

Cast On

Work figure-eight CO with 12 (12, 14, 14) wraps on each of 2 ndls or a closed-toe CO beg with 12 (12, 14, 14) sts. End with 24 (24, 28, 28) sts total after finished CO and ndls in working order for knitting in the round. Divide sts as follows: 6-12-6 (6-12-6; 7-14-7; 7-14-7).

Toe Increases

Rnd 1 (inc rnd): *Ndl 1:* knit to last 2 sts, K1, M1L, K1; *ndl 2:* K1, M1R, knit to last 2 sts, K1, M1L, K1; ndl 3: K1, M1R, knit rem sts (4 sts inc).

Rnd 2: Knit even.

Rep rnds 1 and 2, inc 4 sts EOR until you have a total of 48 (60, 68, 80) sts.

Next rnd on 48 and 68 sts only: *Ndl 1:* knit to last 2 sts, K1, M1L, K1; *ndl 2:* knit; *ndl 3:* K1, M1R, knit rem sts (2 sts inc).

All sizes: You should have a total of 50 (60, 70, 80) sts. Divide sts as follows: 13-24-13; (15-30-15; 18-34-18; 20-40-20).

Foot

Knit all rnds until sock fits just to bottom of ankle bone or until sock foot measures approx 2" less than total length of foot from heel to longest toe.

Gusset Increases and Instep

Rnd 1: *Ndl 1:* knit to last 2 sts, K1, M1L, K1; *ndl 2:* knit all sts; *ndl 3:* K1, M1R, knit rem sts.

Rnd 2: Knit even.

Rep rnds 1 and 2, inc 1 st EOR on each side of heel until gusset section equals 10 (12, 12, 14) sts on each side of heel, ending with a rnd 2: 23 (27, 30, 34) on each of back ndls 1 and 3.

Knit sts on ndls 1 and 2, knit the 10 (12, 12, 14) gusset sts on ndl 3. Pm on beg of ndl 2, slip the 10 (12, 12, 14) gusset sts from ndl 1 onto ndl 2. Pm onto end of ndl 2, slip the 10 (12, 12, 14) gusset sts from ndl 3 onto ndl 2. Now split sts on ndl 2 onto 2 ndls.

Note: Rather than placing gusset sts onto ends of ndl 2, you can use 2 st holders.

Heel

Knit heel sts on ndl 3 and, using same ndl, cont knitting across ndl 1 sts, turn. Beg working back and forth on heel sts only.

Heel Turn

Row 1: Purl across heel sts to last 2 sts, wyib sl 1 st from LH ndl to RH ndl, wyif sl same st back to LH ndl, turn.

Row 2: Knit across heel sts to last 2 sts, wyif sl 1 st from LH ndl to RH ndl, wyib sl same st back to LH ndl, turn.

Row 3: Purl to last 4 sts, slip and wrap next st as in row 1, turn.

Row 4: Knit across to last 4 sts, slip and wrap next st as in row 2, turn.

Cont to work heel sts, dec 2 sts but wrapping only 1 st each row, until you have 8 (10, 12, 14) center sts rem that are knit and 9 (10, 12, 13) sts that are wrapped on each side of center sts.

Note: For first and fourth sizes, on last 2 rows dec 1 st rather than 2 sts.

Heel Increases

When working sts with wraps, work st and wrap tog as 1 st. Refer to "Heel Increases" on page 20 as needed.

Row 1: Purl across center 8 (10, 12, 14) sts, purl across all slipped and wrapped stitches up to last heel st. Purl last heel st tog with 1 gusset st from front needle. Do not wrap next gusset stitch. Turn.

Row 2: Knit back across heel sts, knitting all slipped and wrapped stitches up to last heel st. Knit last heel st tog with 1 gusset st from front needle. Do not wrap next gusset stitch. Turn.

Heel Flap

Row 1: Sl 1, purl across to last heel st, purl last heel st tog with 1 gusset st from front needle. Do not wrap next gusset st, turn.

Row 2: *Sl 1, K1, rep from * across to last heel st, knit last heel st tog with 1 gusset st from front needle. Do not wrap next gusset st. Turn.

Rep rows 1 and 2 until you have incorporated all gusset sts into the heel. Do not turn on last rnd. You should have the same number of sts you began with: 50 (60, 70, 80) sts.

Beg working in the rnd. Return front foot sts to 1 needle, split back heel sts onto 2 ndls.

Next rnd: Knit front foot (instep) sts, knit all heel sts.

Next rnd: Knit front foot (instep) sts, *sl 1, K1, rep from * across all heel sts on ndls 3 and 1.

Rep last 2 rnds once more, then work 1 rnd, knitting all sts, increasing 2 sts on first and third sizes.

Leg and Cuff

Ndl 2 will now be beg of your patt work. Divide sts as follows: 15-20-15 (15-30-15; 20-30-20; 20-40-20). Pm on ndl 2 to mark beg of rnds. Do not work tightly; keep your work slightly loose, but not sloppy.

Rnds 1–3: *(Sl 1, K1) twice, sl 1, K5, rep from * around.

Rnd 4: Knit all sts, lifting the 3 bars behind each slipped st and knitting them with the slipped st as follows: sl the sl st kw to RH ndl, with RH ndl, lift the 3 bars behind sl st, insert LH ndl into front of work and knit bars and sl st tog as 1 st.

Rep rnds 1–4 until leg reaches 7" from bottom curve of heel or to desired height, ending with rnd 4 of patt.

Work in K2, P2 rib for 1½".

Finishing

Bind off *loosely*. Weave in all ends.

Detail of ruching effect, shown in an alternate colorway.

Tropical Breeze

The lovely lacework on the leg of this sock creates an effect similar to a lattice or braided lace. The patterning works especially well for variegated yarns. Whatever yarn you choose, you'll really want to show off these socks.

Finished Size

Circ. of foot (unstretched): 6⅝ (7½, 8⅜, 9¼)"
Circ. of leg (unstretched): 6⅝ (7½, 8⅜, 9¼)"
Height from floor to cuff: approx 7"

Materials

1 skein of Sockotta from Plymouth Yarn (45% cotton/40% Superwash
    wool/15% nylon; 414 yds/379 m; 3.5 oz/100 g), color 30 **1**
Size US 1½ (2.5 mm) double-pointed needles or size to achieve gauge
2 stitch holders (optional)
2 stitch markers
Tapestry needle

Gauge

9 sts = 1" in St st

Cast On

Work figure-eight CO with 10 (12, 12, 14) wraps on each of 2 ndls *or* a closed-toe CO beg with 10 (12, 12, 14) sts. End with 20 (24, 24, 28) sts total after finished CO and ndls in working order for knitting in the round. Divide sts as follows: 5-10-5 (6-12-6; 6-12-6; 7-14-7).

Toe Increases

Rnd 1 (inc rnd): *Ndl 1:* knit to last 2 sts, K1, M1L, K1; *ndl 2:* K1, M1R, knit to last 2 sts, K1, M1L, K1; *ndl 3:* K1, M1R, knit rem sts (4 sts inc).

Rnd 2: Knit even.

Rep rnds 1 and 2, inc 4 sts EOR, until you have a total of 60 (68, 76, 84) sts. Divide as follows: 15-30-15 (17-34-17; 19-38-19; 21-42-21) or until toe fits foot snugly but not tightly just to base of little toe. (If custom fitting your socks, use a multiple of 4 sts).

Foot

Knit all rnds until sock fits just to bottom of ankle bone or until sock foot measures approx 2" less than total length of foot from heel to longest toe.

Gusset Increases and Instep

Rnd 1: *Ndl 1:* knit to last 2 sts, K1, M1L, K1; *ndl 2:* knit all sts; *ndl 3:* K1, M1R, knit rem sts.

Rnd 2: Knit even.

Rep rnds 1 and 2, inc 1 st on each side of heel, until gusset section equals 12 (12, 14, 14) sts on each side of heel, ending with a rnd 2: 27 (29, 33, 35) sts on each of ndls 1 and 3.

Knit sts on ndls 1 and 2, K12 (12, 14, 14) gusset sts on ndl 3. Pm on beg of ndl 2, slip 12 (12, 14, 14) gusset sts from ndl 1 onto ndl 2. Pm onto end of ndl 2, slip the 12 (12, 14, 14) gusset sts from ndl 3 onto ndl 2. Now split sts on ndl 2 onto 2 ndls.

Note: Rather than placing gusset sts onto ends of ndl 2, you can put them on 2 st holders.

Heel

Knit heel sts on ndl 3 and, using same ndl, cont knitting across ndl 1 sts, turn. Beg working back and forth on heel stitches only.

Heel Turn

Row 1: Purl across heel sts to last 2 sts, wyib sl 1 st from LH ndl to RH ndl, wyif sl same st back to LH ndl, turn.

Row 2: Knit across heel sts to last 2 sts, wyif sl 1 st from LH ndl to RH ndl, wyib sl same st back to LH ndl, turn.

Row 3: Purl to last 4 sts, slip and wrap next st as in row 1, turn.

Row 4: Knit across to last 4 sts, slip and wrap next st as in row 2, turn.

Cont to work heel sts, dec 2 sts but wrapping only 1 st each row, until you have 10 (12, 12, 14) center sts rem that are knit and 10 (11, 13, 14) sts that are wrapped on each side of center sts.

Note: For second and third sizes, on last 2 rows dec 1 st rather than 2 sts.

Heel Increases

When working sts with wraps, work st and wrap tog as 1 st. Refer to "Heel Increases" on page 20 as needed.

Row 1: Purl across center 10 (11, 13, 14) sts, purl across all slipped and wrapped sts up to last heel st. Purl last heel st tog with 1 gusset st from front needle. Do not wrap next gusset st. Turn.

Row 2: Knit back across heel sts, knitting all slipped and wrapped sts up to last heel st. Knit last heel st tog with 1 gusset st from front needle. Do not wrap next gusset st. Turn.

Heel Flap

Row 1: Sl 1, purl across to last heel st, purl last heel st tog with 1 gusset st from front ndl. Do not wrap next gusset st, turn.

Row 2: *Sl 1, K1,* rep from * to * across to last heel st, knit last heel st tog with 1 gusset st from front ndl. Do not wrap next gusset st. Turn.

Rep rows 1 and 2 until you have incorporated all gusset sts into the heel. Do not turn on last rnd.

You should have the same number of sts you began with: 60 (68, 76, 84) sts.

Beg working in the rnd. Return front foot sts to 1 ndl, split back heel sts onto 2 ndls.

Next rnd: Knit front foot sts, knit all heel sts.

Next rnd: Knit front foot sts, *sl 1, K1, rep from * across all heel sts on ndls 3 and 1.

Rep last 2 rnds once more, then knit 1 rnd on all sts.

Leg and Cuff

Ndl 2 will now be beg of your patt work. Move 1 st from each end of ndl 2 onto ndls 1 and 3 so sts are divided as follows: 16-28-16 (18-32-18; 20-36-20; 22-40-22). Pm on ndl 2 to mark beg of rnds.

Rnds 1 and 2: Knit. (**Note:** Do not work the knit rnds too tightly or you will have problems working the K2tog in rnd 3.)

Rnd 3: *YO, K2tog, rep from * around.

Rnd 4: Purl.

Rnd 5: Knit.

Rep rnds 3–5 until leg reaches 6½" from bottom of heel or to desired height, ending with patt rnd 5.

Work in K2, P2 rib for 1½".

Finishing

Bind off *loosely*. Weave in all ends.

Changing the Playing Field

The many self-patterning yarns on the market open the opportunity to use more than just stockinette stitch when knitting your socks. This sock will bring out your inner designer and have you playing with colors and stitches to "change the playing field" of self-patterning or striping yarn.

Finished Size

Circ. of foot (unstretched): 6½ (7⅜, 8¼, 9)"
Circ. of leg (unstretched): 6½ (7⅜, 8¼, 9)"
Height from floor to cuff: approx 7"

Materials

1 skein of Cotton from Opal (38% Superwash wool/32% polyamide/30% cotton; 105 yds/96 m; 1.75 oz/50 g), color 2091 (**1**)
Size US 1½ (2.50 mm) double-pointed needles or size to achieve gauge
Stitch holder (optional)
Tapestry needle

Gauge

8.75 sts = 1" in St st

Pattern Notes

The sock shown was worked with yarn from the outside of the skein, not pulled from the inside so that I could easily see where the color changes would occur. While knitting the foot, patterning is worked on front foot stitches only. Bottom of foot is knit in stockinette stitch. After heel is completed, patterning extends around entire leg.

Work each stitch pattern until color changes to next color in repeating sequence of yarn. While working the foot, if color changes at midpoint or toward the end of needle 2, continue in current pattern to end of needle 2. When working the leg, begin each new pattern with either needle 2 or 3.

Stitch Patterns

Don't begin patterning until all toe increases have been completed. Stitch patterns are worked the same for the foot and leg sections unless otherwise noted. If custom fitting your sock, use a multiple of 8 sts.

Patt 1: Stockinette Stitch
Knit all stitches to next color change.

Patt 2: Seed Stitch
Rnd 1: *K1, P1, rep from * around.

Rnd 2: *P1, K1, rep from * around.

Rep rnds 1 and 2 to next color change.

Patt 3: Wide Rib
Worked on front foot stitches only:
All rnds: Knit sts on ndl 1; P2, K4, *P4, K4, rep from * to last 2 sts on ndl 2, P2; knit sts on ndl 3.

Rep rnd to next color change.

Worked on all stitches of the leg:
Beg patt with either ndl 2 or 3.

All rnds: P2, K4, *P4, K4, rep from * around to last 2 sts, P2.

Rep rnd to next color change.

Patt 4: Reverse Stockinette Stitch
Knit 1 rnd for a clean transition between patt, then purl all stitches to next color change.

Patt 5: Slipped Stitch
Worked when only 1 or 2 rnds of white or another CC is present between larger bands of color. After knitting 1 or 2 rnds of white or CC, beg patt st. If desired you can substitute patt 5 with a simple K1, P1 ribbing.

Worked on front foot stitches only:
Rnds 1–3: *Ndl 1*: knit; *ndl 2*: *K3, sl 1 purlwise, rep from * to last 4 sts on ndl, K4; *ndl 3*: knit.

Rnd 4: Knit all sts.

Rep rnd 4 until next color change.

Worked on all stitches of leg:
Beg patt with either ndl 2 or ndl 3.

Rnds 1–3: *K3, sl 1 purlwise, rep from * around.

Rnd 4: Knit all sts.

Rep rnd 4 until next color change.

Color sequence used in model:
Patt 1: Deep blue purple tweed into jacquard
Patt 2: Periwinkle blue and white tweed
Patt 3: Turquoise
Patt 4: Rose
Patt 5: White
Patt 5: Yellow

Cast On

Work figure-eight CO with 12 (12, 14, 14) wraps on each of 2 ndls *or* a closed-toe CO beg with 12 (12, 14, 14) sts. End with 24 (24, 28, 28) sts total after finished CO and with ndls in working order for knitting in the round. Divide sts as follows: 6-12-6 (6-12-6; 7-14-7; 7-14-7).

Toe Increases

Rnd 1 (inc rnd): *Ndl 1:* knit to last 2 sts, K1, M1L, K1; *ndl 2:* K1, M1R, knit to last 2 sts, K1, M1L, K1; *ndl 3:* K1, M1R, knit rem sts (4 sts inc).

Rnd 2: Knit even.

Rep rnds 1 and 2, inc 4 sts EOR, until you have a total of 56 (64, 72, 80) sts. Divide as follows: 14-28-14 (16-32-16; 18-36-18; 20-40-20) *or* until toe fits foot snugly but not tightly just to base of little toe.

Foot

Beg patt on front foot sts, cont to work bottom foot sts in St st until sock fits just to bottom of ankle bone or until sock measures approx 2" less than length of foot from heel to longest toe.

Short-Row Heel Decreases

Row 1: Work across ndl 1 to last 2 sts, wyif sl 1 st from LH ndl to RH ndl, wyib sl same st back to LH ndl. Turn work (wrap and turn complete).

Row 2: Purl across ndl 1 and, using same ndl, purl across ndl 3 to last 2 sts, wyib sl 1 st from LH ndl to RH ndl, wyif sl same st back to LH ndl, turn.

Row 3: Knit to last 3 sts, sl and wrap next st as in row 1, turn.

Row 4: Purl across to last 3 sts, sl and wrap next st as in row 2, turn.

Cont to work heel sts, slipping and wrapping an additional st each row until you have 10 (10, 12, 12) center sts rem that are knit and 9 (11, 12, 14) sts that are wrapped on each side of center sts.

Short-Row Heel Increases

Refer to "Heel Increases" on page 20 as needed.

Row 1: Knit across center 10 (10, 12, 12) sts to closest wrapped st, K1 (knitting st and wrap tog as 1 st), sl and wrap next st, turn.

Row 2: Purl across center 11 (11, 13, 13) sts to closest wrapped st, P1 (purling st and wrap tog as 1 st), sl and wrap next st, turn.

Cont to work heel sts, bringing 1 st back into work each row until you have worked all sts. On last 2 rows, knit across, wrap last st, turn, purl across, wrap last st, turn.

Knit each of these last 2 sts with their wraps tog as 1 st when you come to them on first rnd of leg.

Leg and Cuff

You should have the same number of sts you began with before working heel.

Return front foot sts to 1 needle, split back foot onto 2 needles. If necessary, cut yarn, leaving a 4" to 6" tail, and reattach new section, beg with appropriate color, to keep in color and patt sequence from where you left off before beg of short-row heel.

Work in est color and patt sequence on all sts. Beg each new patt with either ndl 2 or ndl 3 until leg measures 4½" above heel.

Work in K2, P2 rib for 1¾".

Finishing

Bind off *loosely*. Weave in all ends.

Detail of stitch patterns used with self-striping yarn.

Lacy Waves

The lovely lace-and-wave pattern will make these socks one of your favorite pairs. With the lace pattern worked only on the top of the foot and front leg section, they're extremely comfortable as well as being fast and easy to knit.

Finished Size

Circ. of foot (unstretched): 6½ (7½, 8¼)"
Circ. of leg (unstretched): 6½ (7½, 8¼)"
Height from floor to cuff: approx 7"

Materials

1 (1, 2) skeins of Cotton Fleece from Brown Sheep (80% cotton/20% merino
  wool; 215 yds/197 m; 3.5 oz/100 g), color CW-375 Rue [3]
Size US 4 (3.5 mm) double-pointed needles or size to achieve gauge
Stitch holder (optional)
Row counter (optional)
Tapestry needle

Gauge

6.25 sts = 1" in St st

Lace Pattern

Worked across front 18 (20, 22) sts on ndl 2 only. Ndl 1 and 3 are always knit. If custom fitting your sock, use a multiple of 4 sts. Lace patt is worked on 18 center front sts for all sizes.

Rnd 1: Knit.

Rnd 2: Knit.

Rnd 3: K0 (1, 2), K2tog 3 times, (YO, K1) 6 times, K2tog 3 times, K0 (1, 2).

Rnd 4: K0 (1, 2), P18, K0 (1, 2).

Cast On

For all sizes, work figure-eight CO with 8 wraps on each of 2 ndls or a closed-toe CO beg with 8 sts. End with 16 sts total after finished CO and ndls are in working order for knitting in the round. Divide sts as follows: 4-8-4.

Toe Increases

Rnd 1 (inc rnd): *Ndl 1:* knit to last 2 sts, K1, M1L, K1; *ndl 2:* K1, M1R, knit to last 2 sts, K1, M1L, K1; *ndl 3:* K1, M1R, knit rem sts (4 sts inc).

Rnd 2: Knit even.

Rep rnds 1 and 2, inc 4 sts EOR, until you have a total of 36 (40, 44) sts. Divide sts as follows: 9-18-9 (10-20-10; 11-22-11) or until toe fits foot snugly but not tightly just to base of little toe.

Foot

Rnd 1: *Ndl 1:* Knit all sts; *ndl 2:* work rnd 1 of lace patt across 18 (20, 22) sts; *ndl 3:* Knit all sts.

Rnd 2: *Ndl 1:* knit all sts; *ndl 2:* work rnd 2 of lace patt across 18 (20, 22) sts; *ndl 3:* knit all sts.

Rnd 3: *Ndl 1:* knit all sts; *ndl 2:* work rnd 3 of lace patt across 18 (20, 22) sts; *ndl 3:* knit all sts.

Rnd 4: *Ndl 1:* knit all sts; *ndl 2:* work rnd 4 of lace patt across 18 (20, 22) sts; *ndl 3:* knit all sts.

Rep rnds 1–4 until sock reaches ankle bone or measures approx 2" less than total length of foot from heel to longest toe, ending with rnd 4.

Short-Row Heel Decreases

Row 1: Work across ndl 1 to last 2 sts, wyif sl 1 st from LH ndl to RH ndl, wyib sl same st back to LH ndl. Turn work (wrap and turn complete).

Row 2: Purl across ndl 1 and, using same needle, purl across ndl 3 to last 2 sts, wyib sl 1 st from LH ndl to RH ndl, wyif sl same st back to LH ndl, turn.

Row 3: Knit to last 3 sts, sl and wrap next st as in row 1, turn.

Row 4: Purl to last 3 sts, sl and wrap next st as in row 2, turn.

Cont to slip and wrap an additional st each row, until you have 8 center sts that are knit and 5 (6, 7) sts that are wrapped on each side of center sts.

Short-Row Heel Increases

Refer to "Heel Increases" on page 20 as needed.

Row 1: Knit across center 8 sts to closest wrapped st, K1 (knitting st and wrap tog as 1 st), sl and wrap next st, turn.

Row 2: Purl across center 9 sts to closest wrapped st, P1 (purling st and wrap tog as 1 st), sl and wrap next st, turn.

Cont to work heel sts, bringing 1 st back into work each row, until you have worked all sts. On last 2 rows, knit across, wrap last st, turn, purl across, wrap last st, turn. Knit each of these last 2 sts with their wraps tog as 1 st when you come to them on first rnd of leg.

Leg and Cuff

If you placed front sts on a holder, return them to ndl. You should have the same number of sts you began with before working heel.

Rnd 1: *Ndl 3:* knit all sts; *ndl 1:* knit all sts; work rnd 1 of lace patt across 18 (20, 22) sts on ndl 2; knit all sts on ndl 3.

You will now work in rnds on 3 ndls. Cont in est patt as for foot (with next rnd being rnd 2) until you have 7 reps on leg, ending with rnd 4.

Work in K2, P2 rib for 1¾".

Finishing

Bind off *loosely*. Weave in all ends.

Pedi Socks

These short little socks are great for showing off your pedicure and adding pizzazz to summer thongs and sandals. They feel great on your feet, giving a little added comfort for thong wearers. They're so fun, you'll want to make them in a rainbow of colors.

Finished Size

To fit shoe sizes: 4–5 (5½–6½; 7–8; 8½–9½; 10–11)
Circ. of foot (unstretched): 5¾ (6½, 7⅛, 7⅞, 8½)"
Length: 2¾ (3, 3¼, 3½, 3¾)"

Materials

1 skein of Regia Stretch Color from Schachenmayr Nomotta (70% new
wool/23% polyamide/7% polyester; 221 yds/200 m; 1.75 oz/50 g),
color 0082 Fantasie Color ⟨1⟩

Alternate yarn: 1 skein of Clown from Marks & Kattens (45% cotton/40%
Superwash wool/15% nylon; 208 yds/190 m; 1.75 oz/50 g), color 1720
or 1907 ⟨1⟩

6 size US 1½ (2.5 mm) double-pointed needles or size to achieve gauge *or* 1
set of US 1½ (2.5 mm) double-pointed needles and 2 small stitch holders

1 stitch marker

Tapestry needle

Gauge

8.5 sts = 1" in St st

Right Pedi Sock

Big-Toe Section

CO 22 (24, 26, 28, 30) sts and
divide onto 3 ndls as follows: 5-9-8
(5-10-9; 6-11-9; 6-12-10; 7-13-10).
Pm between first and second sts on
ndl 1 and sl marker with each rnd.

Rnds 1–10: Knit.

Rnd 11: Knit sts on ndls 1 and 2,
BO first 4 sts on ndl 3 for bridge
between toes, K1, sl rem unworked
sts onto RH ndl. Sl sts from ndl 1
(including marker) onto ndl 3: 9 (10,
11, 12, 13) sts on ndl 3. Keep 9 (10,
11, 12, 13) sts on ndl 2.

Note: In place of 2 dpns, you can
place toe sts onto 2 small st holders.

Cut yarn, leaving a 6" tail, and set
big-toe section aside.

Remaining-Toes Section

CO 28 (32, 36, 40, 44) sts and
divide onto 3 ndls as follows: 6-16-6
(7-18-7; 8-20-8; 9-22-9; 10-24-10).

Rnds 1 and 2: Knit.

Rnd 3 (inc rnd): *Ndl 1:* knit; *ndl 2:* knit to last 2 sts, K1, M1L, K1; *ndl 3:* K1, M1R, knit rem sts (2 sts inc).

Rnd 4: Knit.

Rnds 5–8: Rep rnds 3 and 4: 34 (38, 42, 46, 50) sts.

Rnd 9: *Ndl 1:* knit; *ndl 2:* BO 4 sts for bridge between toes, knit to last 2 sts, K1, M1L, K1; *ndl 3:* K1, M1R, knit rem sts: 32 (36, 40, 44, 48) sts.

Rnd 10: *Ndl 1:* knit; with same ndl, K9 (10, 11, 12, 13) big-toe sts from ndl with marker. With empty ndl, K9 (10, 11, 12, 13) rem big-toe sts, then with same ndl, knit sts on ndl 2 of rem-toes section; *ndl 3:* knit: 50 (56, 62, 68, 74) sts.

Foot and Cuff

Work even until piece measures 2¼ (2½, 2¾, 3, 3¼)" from beg of partial foot section (exclude big toe) or sock measures ½" shorter than length desired.

Work K1, P1 ribbing for 8 rnds.

Finishing

Bind off *loosely*. Sew gap closed on bridge between toes. Weave in all ends.

Left Pedi Sock

Left sock is worked as for right sock with reverse shaping as follows.

Big-Toe Section

CO 22 (24, 26, 28, 30) sts and divide onto 3 ndls as follows: 5-13-4 (5-14-5; 6-15-5; 6-16-6; 7-17-6).

Pm between first and second sts on ndl 1 and sl marker with each rnd.

Rnds 1–10: Knit.

Rnd 11: *Ndl 1:* knit; *ndl 2:* BO 4 sts for bridge between toes, knit rem sts; *ndl 3:* K3, sl rem sts onto RH ndl. Sl sts from ndl 1 (including marker) onto ndl 3: 9 (10, 11, 12, 13) sts. Keep 9 (10, 11, 12, 13) sts on ndl 2.

Cut yarn, leaving a 6" tail, and set big-toe section aside.

Remaining-Toes Section

Reverse shaping from right sock, inc on ndls 1 and 2. The bridge bind off is worked at beg of ndl 3.

CO 28 (32, 36, 40, 44) sts and divide onto 3 ndls as follows: 6-12-10 (7-14-11; 8-16-12; 9-18-13; 10-20-14).

Work as for right sock, inc EOR at end of ndl 1 and beg of ndl 2 to rnd 9.

Rnd 9: *Ndl 1:* knit to last 2 sts, K1, M1L, K1; *ndl 2:* K1, M1R, knit rem sts; *ndl 3:* BO 4 sts, knit rem sts: 32 (36, 40, 44, 48) sts.

Rnd 10: *Ndl 1:* knit; *ndl 2:* knit; with same ndl, K9 (10, 11, 12) big-toe sts from ndl *without* marker. With empty ndl, K9 (10, 11, 12) rem big-toe sts (set with marker), then with same ndl, knit sts on ndl 3 and remove marker: 50 (56, 62, 68, 74) sts.

Finishing

Work foot and cuff and finish as for right sock.

Pedi socks knit in alternate colorways using Clown from Marks & Kattens.

Abbreviations

approx	approximately		P	purl
beg	begin(ning)		pm	place marker
BO	bind off		patt	pattern
CO	cast on		psso	pass slipped stitch over
circ	circumference		rem	remain(ing)
cont	continue, continuing		rep	repeat
dec	decrease(d), decreasing		RH	right-hand
dpn(s)	double-pointed needle(s)		rnd	round
est	established		st(s)	stitch(es)
EOR	every other row or round		sl	slip
g	gram(s)		ssk	slip 1 stitch as if to knit, slip 1 more stitch as if to knit, return stitches to left needle and knit them together (1 stitch decreased)
inc	increase(d), increasing			
K	knit			
K2tog	knit 2 stitches together (1 stitch decreased)			
LH	left-hand			
m	meter(s)		tog	together
M1L	increase 1 stitch using left-slanting increase		wyib	with yarn in back
			wyif	with yarn in front
M1R	increase 1 stitch using right-slanting increase		yds	yards
			YO	yarn over needle
ndl(s)	needle(s)			

Yarn Weights

Yarn-Weight Symbol and Category Name	0 LACE	1 SUPER FINE	2 FINE	3 LIGHT
Types of Yarn in Category	Fingering, 10-count crochet thread	Sock, Fingering, Baby	Sport, Baby	DK, Light Worsted
Knit Gauge Range* in Stockinette Stitch to 4"	33 to 40 sts	27 to 32 sts	23 to 26 sts	21 to 24 sts
Recommended Needle in U.S. Size Range	000 to 1	1 to 3	3 to 5	5 to 7
Recommended Needle in Metric Size Range	1.5 to 2.25 mm	2.25 to 3.25 mm	3.25 to 3.75 mm	3.75 to 4.5 mm

These are guidelines only. The above reflect the most commonly used gauges and needle sizes for specific yarn categories.

Resources

Brown Sheep Co., Inc.
(308) 635-2198
www.brownsheep.com
Cotton Fleece

Cascade Yarns
(206) 574-0440
www.cascadeyarns.com
Fixation

Cherry Tree Hill
(802) 525-3311
www.cherryyarn.com
Sockittome

Fiesta Yarns
(505) 892-5008
www.fiestayarns.com
Baby Boom

Patons Yarn
(416) 782-2969
Kroy Socks

Plymouth Yarn Company, Inc.
(215) 788-0459
www.plymouthyarn.com
Sockotta

Swedish Yarn Imports
(800) 331-5648
www.swedishyarn.com
Distributor for Marks & Kattens's *Clown*

TUTTO Opal-Isager
(877) 603-6725
www.opalsockyarn.com
Distributor for *Opal Cotton*

Westminster Fibers, Inc.
(800) 445-9276
www.westminsterfibers.com
Distributor for Schachenmayr Nomotta's *Regia Stretch* and *Regia Bamboo*

Acknowledgments

There are many people that I owe a great deal to and although I will never be able to thank them enough for their help and contributions, I would like to recognize some very special people.

Karen Soltys, acquisitions and development editor. Thank you for allowing this book to again see the light of day. Working with Martingale & Company is always such a wonderful experience, and I was so happy the day you called wanting to expand and republish this book. Your suggestions and revamping of my verbiage has greatly improved my work and made it easier for knitters to follow.

Cathy Reitan, author liaison. Thank you for all your help and for keeping things rolling smoothly.

Hayden and Mari Creque. Thank you for supporting the underdog. Hayden, you rock! And Mari, here's to the most underpaid but highly appreciated secretary I've ever known. Keep that copy machine running, honey.

Timothy Maher, illustrator. Tim created our illustrations to be realistic and true to life so that you as a knitter could visualize and work with my instructions. Tim, your patience is overwhelming and I thank you so much for all your hard work. Without you this book would not be what it is. I'll bet you know more about the flow of knit stitches than you ever wanted to. Aren't you glad we met on the bike path?

Patricia Simkowski, Rozetta (Bee) Hahn, and Lois Blanchard. Thank you for proofing text and for knitting several of the models for this book. Without you—my three wonder knitters—I'd be up the proverbial creek. I love you guys!

Meet the Author and Illustrator

Janet Rehfeldt has been knitting and crocheting since the age of seven. She is the owner of Knitted Threads Designs and is an instructor, a designer, and an author. Her designs can be found in leading knitting and crochet publications. She is the author of *Crocheted Socks: 16 Fun-to-Stitch Patterns* from Martingale & Company, and she teaches on both a local and national level. Janet lives in Sun Prairie, Wisconsin, with her husband.

Tim Maher has a bachelor's degree from the University of Illinois in industrial design and is the principal of Twin Dog Design. His previous illustration and design work includes training materials for the nuclear industry and toy design. After becoming a stay-at-home dad for three children, Tim pursued freelance graphic-design work, which led to illustration and design for numerous crafts publications. In addition, he has created illustrations, logo designs, and cover art for various clients. He lives with his family in Florida.